Dear Mark,

I hope this little book will be a
source of hope and encouragement
at all times, as God's presence is.
My thoughts and prayers are with
you dear Brother.
 Dave.

Lit
Prom~~ises~~

GW00399932

HOPE and
ENCOURAGEMENT from

Our Daily Bread

Compiled by Dave Branon

Our Daily Bread
Publishing™

Introduction

I love pithy, memorable quotes—whether they come from movies, sports figures, or famous politicians. When money is the subject, I like to quote George Bailey in *It's a Wonderful Life*. When the angel Clarence confessed to George that in heaven they didn't know anything about money, George opined: "It comes in pretty handy down here, Bub." And indeed it does.

When I consider an ache or pain that might stop me from doing what I want to do, I think of Hall of Famer Sparky Anderson, manager of my two favorite baseball teams, the Cincinnati Reds and the Detroit Tigers. Sparky, trying to downplay the injury of one of his players, declared, "Pain don't hurt!" Well, yes it does, Sparky, but I think we know what you are trying to say.

And what American does not admire the words of Martin Luther King Jr., who told the masses on the steps of the Lincoln Memorial on August 28, 1963, "I have a dream that my four little children will one day live in a nation where they will not be judged by the color of their skin, but by the content of their character"? We're still working on it, Dr. King.

Since 1956, this ministry has produced a little booklet called *Our Daily Bread*. Every day since April 1 of that year, people around the United States and later all over the world have read the words our writers have used to encourage salvation in Jesus Christ, foster spiritual growth through a better understanding of Scripture, and call for greater devotion to our great God. The writers have always worked hard to make their words powerful—using a small format to express timeless truths.

As a result, the devotional articles often generate memorable sayings—quotes full of valuable truths and applicable teachings. For example, for the entry on June 19, 1956, Henry Bosch, the first editor of *Our Daily Bread*, wrote, "As we feed on the written Word, we will become more conformed to the Living Word." Profound, simple, and helpful.

Move ahead to the July 1956 edition, and you read this from the founder of what was then called Radio Bible Class (now Our Daily Bread Ministries), Dr. M. R. DeHaan: "We walk by faith in Him who can give strength for the way and can lead us around or carry us over the obstacles ahead."

There is encouragement in these short, truth-packed lines from the original pages of *Our Daily Bread*.

Several years ago we produced our first collection of memorable sayings from *Our Daily Bread,* and it was called *Small Blessings.* My favorite saying from that edition was written by Cindy Hess Kasper: "Life, love, and chocolate taste better when shared with others." I like the warmth of that thought—and I love chocolate. And Herb Vander Lugt said, "Keep a wide gulf between yourself and your possessions." In an age of consumerism, we all need that reminder.

And now we come to our second collection: *Little Promises.* Again, it has been our joy to scan the pages of *Our Daily Bread* to glean sayings and epithets that capture the essence of biblical truth. In these pages you'll find encouragement to love God more, to serve others better, and to grow stronger in your walk with your Savior.

I will leave you with one more saying that epitomizes my prayer for you—and it comes from the pen of my friend and former *Our Daily Bread* writer Dr. Dennis Fisher: "Wherever we are and whatever we're doing, God wants to be a part of it." I hope that thought and this book can encourage you as you take steps each day in your journey with God along the way to heaven.

Dave Branon
Compiler

Every moment in God's presence provides a breathtaking revelation of His beauty and love.

JAMES BANKS

Because your love is better than life,
my lips will glorify you.

PSALM 63:3

What we call an interruption may be a divine appointment the Lord has scheduled for this day.

DAVID MCCASLAND

Jesus asked him, "What do you want me to do for you?" "Lord, I want to see," he replied.

LUKE 18:40–41

Enjoy the bright splashes and breathtaking beauty in the world around us. It's a small foretaste of the "paradise" to come.

ALYSON KIEDA

He who was seated on the throne said, "I am making everything new!"

REVELATION 21:5

As our loving Father helps us, He empowers us to reach out to others in need, affirming they too aren't alone.

XOCHITL DIXON

Since we are surrounded by such a great cloud of witnesses . . . let us run with perseverance the race marked out for us.

HEBREWS 12:1

What an amazing thing it would be if people could observe us and say, "I see Jesus in you"!

DAVE BRANON

We all . . . are being transformed into his image with ever-increasing glory, which comes from the Lord, who is the Spirit.

2 CORINTHIANS 3:18

When we serve
the Lord, no job
or act of love
is too menial
to matter.

XOCHITL DIXON

Nothing you do for the Lord
is ever useless.

1 CORINTHIANS 15:58 NLT

Just as the sun burns away a fog, our faith in God can burn away the haze of doubt.

CINDY HESS KASPER

Now faith is confidence in what we hope for and assurance about what we do not see.

HEBREWS 11:1

God is present;
God is strong; He's looked
after us in the past
and will do so again.

SHERIDAN VOYSEY

Look to the Lord and his strength;
seek his face always.

1 CHRONICLES 16:11

We don't get spiritual blessings because we're strong; we get them because we believe in Jesus. These blessings come only through God's undeserved grace!

KEILA OCHOA

By grace you have been saved.

EPHESIANS 2:5

Cast your burden on Him. He is the Prince of Peace, and He has promised to send tranquility.

DAVID EGNER

The LORD gives strength to his people; the LORD blesses his people with peace.

PSALM 29:11

Jesus, our Advocate, can turn a prison of lost hope, fear, or regret into the place of His presence.

MART DEHAAN

If anybody does sin, we have an advocate with the Father—Jesus Christ, the Righteous One.

1 JOHN 2:1

When we remember who God is and how much He loves us, we can relax into His peace.

KEILA OCHOA

I sought the LORD, and he answered me; he delivered me from all my fears.

PSALM 34:4

Humility is the right response to God's holiness. And praise is our heart's response to His forgiveness.

JENNIFER BENSON SCHULDT

A broken and contrite heart you, God, will not despise.

PSALM 51:17

There's no telling what a simple act of kindness done in Jesus's name can do.

TIM GUSTAFSON

Religion that God our Father accepts as pure and faultless is this: to look after orphans and widows in their distress.

JAMES 1:27

If we have a generous attitude about money, we are much more likely to be generous in other matters concerning the Lord's people and His work.

MARVIN WILLIAMS

It is hard for someone who is rich to enter the kingdom of heaven.

MATTHEW 19:23

When we call on the name of Jesus, He can enable us to believe and rely on the power of His presence.

XOCHITL DIXON

"'If you can'?" said Jesus. "Everything is possible for one who believes."

MARK 9:23

God sweeps sin itself away, inviting us to return to Him for our clean new life.

PATRICIA RAYBON

I have swept away your offenses
like a cloud, your sins like the morning mist.

ISAIAH 44:22

God's Word is our divine defense!

JENNIFER BENSON SCHULDT

Take . . . the sword of the Spirit, which
is the word of God.

EPHESIANS 6:17

Spending time with Jesus will help us spread a pleasing fragrance to those around us.

MARION STROUD

We are to God the pleasing aroma of Christ.

2 CORINTHIANS 2:15

Life is messy, but God is greater than the mess.

DAVID MCCASLAND

You, LORD, are my lamp;
the LORD turns my darkness
into light.

2 SAMUEL 22:29

God hasn't just left the porch light on for us. He's out on the front porch watching, waiting, calling us home.

JAMES BANKS

While he was still a long way off, his father saw him and was filled with compassion for him.

LUKE 15:20

Clinging to God's
promises in hard
times strengthens
our faith.

DAVID MCCASLAND

I am coming soon. Hold on
to what you have.

REVELATION 3:11

No matter how dark
the night, the unseen
God is ready to
respond appropriately
to our need.

DAVID EGNER

I AM WHO I AM.

EXODUS 3:14

If we show Jesus's beauty with our lives, others will say, "No wonder you love Him!"

KEILA OCHOA

We love Him because
He first loved us.

1 JOHN 4:19 NKJV

Let the world you inhabit inspire you to worship the One who owns it.

JENNIFER BENSON SCHULDT

The earth is the LORD's,
and everything in it.

PSALM 24:1

Sometimes God uses unexpected encounters to bring unexpected blessings.

ANNE CETAS

The LORD repay your work, and
a full reward be given you by
the LORD God of Israel.

RUTH 2:12 NKJV

Forgiveness and grace are always available to the spiritual traveler.

DENNIS FISHER

Let us lay aside every weight, and the
sin which so easily ensnares us, and
let us run with endurance the race
that is set before us.

HEBREWS 12:1 NKJV

Praise is our enthusiastic expression of gratitude to God for reigning in glory forever.

JULIE ACKERMAN LINK

Praise the LORD.

PSALM 150:1

God can create
roads where
we see only
obstacles.

DAVID MCCASLAND

Your path led through the sea, your
way through the mighty waters.

PSALM 77:19

Serving our great God with His strength in a small way is not a stepping-stone to greatness—it *is* greatness.

DAVID ROPER

Who dares despise the day
of small things?

ZECHARIAH 4:10

God's love is a beacon of hope— our ever-present, inexhaustible source of strength and confidence.

JOE STOWELL

Your love, LORD, reaches to the heavens, your faithfulness to the skies.

PSALM 36:5

Because God always remains the same, we can rely on Him through the shifting seasons of life.

JENNIFER BENSON SCHULDT

There is a time for everything.

ECCLESIASTES 3:1

Stay connected to Jesus. He alone can satisfy your thirsty soul!

JOE STOWELL

Let anyone who is thirsty
come to me and drink.

JOHN 7:37

A good plan for our lives today: Receive love. Give love. Repeat.

ANNE CETAS

We have known and believed the love
that God has for us. God is love.

1 JOHN 4:16 NKJV

Think of the challenges you face. Then write this beside each as a reminder of the Lord's care: "For this, I have Jesus."

MARION STROUD

The LORD comforts his people and will have compassion on his afflicted ones.

ISAIAH 49:13

We honor God
when we make
reconciliation with
others a priority.

DAVE BRANON

Be reconciled to your brother.

MATTHEW 5:24 NKJV

No matter how bleak the landscape of life may look, God can transform it into a glorious garden of color and fragrance.

JULIE ACKERMAN LINK

The LORD blessed the latter part of Job's life more than the former part.

JOB 42:12

The mark of true, godly leadership is not power and privilege, but humble service.

DAVID MCCASLAND

Whoever wants to be first must be slave of all.

MARK 10:44

What is the heart? A deep void within us that only God can fill.

DAVID ROPER

[God] has . . . set eternity
in the human heart.

ECCLESIASTES 3:11

Like a creative leather product created by a skilled craftsman's hands, we are each beautiful and valuable simply because we are God's one-of-a-kind creations.

XOCHITL DIXON

You knit me together in
my mother's womb.

PSALM 139:13

Although we recoil at the thought of dying, we can embrace with joy the promise of eternity.

AMY BOUCHER PYE

The throne of God and of the Lamb
will be in the city, and his servants will
serve him. They will see his face.

REVELATION 22:3-4

The joy God provides through the things He has done for us should bring a smile to our face.

DAVE BRANON

The prospect of the righteous is joy.

PROVERBS 10:28

Only God can bring ultimate significance to our most tragic events.

TIM GUSTAFSON

How long, LORD? Will you
forget me forever? . . .
But I trust in your unfailing love.

PSALM 13:1, 5

As the Holy Spirit enables us to obey God's Word, we can avoid the searing sin that separates us from the abundant life God promises.

XOCHITL DIXON

Since we live by the Spirit, let us keep in step with the Spirit.

GALATIANS 5:25

What is love? God is love, and He has poured out that love on you and me.

ANNE CETAS

This is love: not that we loved God, but that he loved us and sent his Son as an atoning sacrifice for our sins.

1 JOHN 4:10

Our faith is rooted in the well-documented life of Jesus, who came to give us peace with God. His story stands.

TIM GUSTAFSON

I myself have carefully investigated everything from the beginning.

LUKE 1:3

Life will have its difficulties, but our Savior, who loves us more than life itself, is greater than them all.

JAMES BANKS

Peace I leave with you; my peace I give you. I do not give to you as the world gives. Do not let your hearts be troubled and do not be afraid.

JOHN 14:27

There are no soloists in God's orchestra. The music is most majestic when we each play our part in unity with others.

DAVID MCCASLAND

So in Christ we, though many, form one body, and each member belongs to all the others. We have different gifts, according to the grace given to each of us.

ROMANS 12:5-6

It may surprise us to consider that God doesn't need us to defend Him. He wants us to *represent* Him!

TIM GUSTAFSON

A gentle answer turns away wrath, but a harsh word stirs up anger.

PROVERBS 15:1

Isn't it comforting to know that God cares enough to listen to all of our prayers—from the shortest to the longest?

JAMES BANKS

The LORD is near to all who call on him, to all who call on him in truth.

PSALM 145:18

If you are controlled by the love of the Lord Jesus, your prayers, kindness, and generous spirit will likewise make you a fragrant Christian!

HERB VANDER LUGT

Mary took about a pint of pure nard, an expensive perfume; she poured it on Jesus' feet and wiped his feet with her hair.

JOHN 12:3

When we call on God to help us in our trouble, the most difficult situations we face can become doorways to a deeper relationship with Him.

DAVID MCCASLAND

When I am in distress, I call to you, because you answer me.

PSALM 86:7

The cross is the inexpressibly wonderful evidence of God's love for us.

DENNIS FISHER

"He himself bore our sins" in his body on the cross.

1 PETER 2:24

Remaining true to Jesus may be difficult, discouraging, and even dangerous, but it is never pointless or wasted.

DAVID MCCASLAND

Therefore, my dear brothers and sisters, stand firm. Let nothing move you. Always give yourselves fully to the work of the Lord, because you know that your labor in the Lord is not in vain.

1 CORINTHIANS 15:58

What's the best gift we can give God today? In gratitude, humility, and love we can give ourselves completely to Him—heart, mind, and will.

DAVID MCCASLAND

Offer your bodies as a living sacrifice, holy and pleasing to God—this is your true and proper worship.

ROMANS 12:1

When we look to the Lord for our sense of peace and well-being, He will fill us with His goodness and love.

AMY BOUCHER PYE

As goods increase, so do those who consume them. And what benefit are they to the owners?

ECCLESIASTES 5:11

The challenges and opportunities we face on our journey can be met confidently, for God has promised us His never-failing presence.

BILL CROWDER

I will not leave you as orphans;
I will come to you.

JOHN 14:18

May we never underestimate the wonder of what it means for anyone, anywhere to hear the good news and say yes to our Savior.

DAVE BRANON

Go into all the world and preach the gospel to all creation.

MARK 16:15

If we remain watchful
and pray—for ourselves
and for others—the
Holy Spirit will enable
us to resist temptation.

KEILA OCHOA

Watch and pray so that you will not
fall into temptation.

MARK 14:38

Let us work with a smile today, remembering that no matter what we are doing, we are serving God.

KEILA OCHOA

God is not unjust; he will not forget your work and the love you have shown him as you have helped his people.

HEBREWS 6:10

Stop and take a breath. Tune out the distractions, put away the restlessness, and reflect on the wonder of God's faithfulness. Get some real rest.

POH FANG CHIA

[Jesus] said to them, "Come with me by yourselves to a quiet place and get some rest."

MARK 6:31

How easy it is to forget that someone right next to us might need a prayer, a word of comfort, a hug, or a gift of mercy in Jesus's name.

DAVE BRANON

We can comfort those in any trouble with the comfort we ourselves receive from God.

2 CORINTHIANS 1:4

Let's work while we can, save what we can, share when we can—and trust God to meet our needs.

JULIE ACKERMAN LINK

Those who work their land will have abundant food.

PROVERBS 12:11

We come to know
God and His wisdom
when we search for it
with our whole heart—
seeking it like hidden
treasure.

CINDY HESS KASPER

Search for [insight and understanding]
as for hidden treasure.

PROVERBS 2:4

Whenever we encounter suffering, may we remember what Jesus endured for us.

LAWRENCE DARMANI

If I must boast, I will boast of the things that show my weakness.

2 CORINTHIANS 11:30

The Lord guides and guards all who walk with Him.

DAVID MCCASLAND

The steps of a good man are ordered by the LORD, and He delights in his way.

PSALM 37:23 NKJV

If we will allow God's work to be done in us, we might be surprised at what He can do through us!

BILL CROWDER

God chose the weak things of the world
to shame the strong.

1 CORINTHIANS 1:27

When we feel inadequate, let's remember this: God asks us to give what we have in faithful obedience. He's the one who makes it "enough."

KIRSTEN HOLMBERG

Be kind to one another, tenderhearted, forgiving one another, even as God in Christ forgave you.

EPHESIANS 4:32 NKJV

When life seems too much
to bear, that's when we
throw ourselves on God's
mercy—and He holds
on to us.

ANNE CETAS

My Father, if it is possible, may this
cup be taken from me.

MATTHEW 26:39

Life can be painful at times, yet God offers His comforting hand in the midst of it. We are never beyond His reach.

DENNIS FISHER

I cling to you; your right hand upholds me.

PSALM 63:8

Our one true source for optimism is that our redemption is in Jesus. He is our reason for hope!

DAVID MCCASLAND

Trust in the LORD and do good.

PSALM 37:3

Like a parent whose arms are a safe retreat from danger, God's comforting presence protects us from life's emotional storms.

LINDA WASHINGTON

He will cover you with his feathers, and under his wings you will find refuge.

PSALM 91:4

When a dad who loves God corrects, comforts, instructs, and provides for his children, he models for them our perfect heavenly Father.

CINDY HESS KASPER

The righteous lead blameless lives;
blessed are their children after them.

PROVERBS 20:7

There is one force that the darkness cannot conquer—the force of loving acts of kindness done in Jesus's name.

JOE STOWELL

Let your light shine before others, that they may see your good deeds and glorify your Father in heaven.

MATTHEW 5:16

We are never too badly broken for God to reshape.

CINDY HESS KASPER

[The vessel] was marred . . . ; so he made it again into another vessel, as it seemed good to the potter to make.

JEREMIAH 18:4 NKJV

We fight the sin of prejudice when we let God's love for us reflect the way we love and treat each other.

MARVIN WILLIAMS

My brothers and sisters, believers in our glorious Lord Jesus Christ must not show favoritism.

JAMES 2:1

In whatever ways the Holy Spirit has gifted you, let Him use you for His glory.

ANNE CETAS

The Advocate, the Holy Spirit, . . .
will teach you all things.

JOHN 14:26

Following Jesus is not turning over a new leaf; it is beginning a new life under a new Master.

MARVIN WILLIAMS

Therefore, if anyone is in Christ, the new creation has come: The old has gone, the new is here!

2 CORINTHIANS 5:17

To show someone loving hospitality just might be the first step in showing that person the way to heaven.

BILL CROWDER

Let the one who is thirsty come; and let the one who wishes take the free gift of the water of life.

REVELATION 22:17

Jesus endured darkness and death to give us light and life. Praise Him for what He went through for us!

DAVID MCCASLAND

As soon as Judas had taken the bread, he went out. And it was night.

JOHN 13:30

When your heart is hurting, present your needs to God. Through Christ, you have full and immediate access to the Father.

BILL CROWDER

Through [Jesus] we have gained access by faith into this grace in which we now stand. And we boast in hope of the glory of God.

ROMANS 5:2

We serve Jesus best
by serving others.
The lower we bend,
the closer we are
to Him.

JAMES BANKS

Those who humble themselves
will be exalted.

MATTHEW 23:12

Whenever we seek safety, it is God's presence with us that provides the strength and protection we need.

ELISA MORGAN

The name of the LORD is a fortified tower;
the righteous run to it and are safe.

PROVERBS 18:10

What a joy it is when people unite to worship together in love—a slice of heaven we can enjoy here on earth!

JOE STOWELL

My command is this: Love each other as I have loved you.

JOHN 15:12

Some of us have made wrong choices, but our past words and deeds need not define our future in God's eyes. There's always a fresh start when we ask for His forgiveness.

CINDY HESS KASPER

I have strayed like a lost sheep.
Seek your servant.

PSALM 119:176

Focusing on who God is rather than on what we think He should do will guide us to joy and satisfaction in Him.

JENNIFER BENSON SCHULDT

When the Israelites saw [the manna], they said to each other, "What is it?"

EXODUS 16:15

Whatever storm we encounter today, we can be confident that all is not lost. Our Pilot can handle the storm. He will get us home.

C. P. HIA

Let us go over to the other side.

MARK 4:35

Look at the very last thing Jesus said in the very last chapter of His book: "Surely I am coming quickly" (Revelation 22:20 NKJV). Today could be the day!

DAVID ROPER

Let your gentleness be evident to all.
The Lord is near.

PHILIPPIANS 4:5

When we give away what the Lord has given to us, He is honored, others are helped, and we are blessed.

DAVID MCCASLAND

I think it is necessary to send back to you Epaphroditus, . . . whom you sent to take care of my needs.

PHILIPPIANS 2:25

When we lose our bearings in life, we can trust our God, who gives His trustworthy Word as our compass.

MARVIN WILLIAMS

Your word is a lamp for my feet,
a light on my path.

PSALM 119:105

No gift giving could ever compete with the Lord's extravagance. Thank God for the indescribable gift of Jesus!

ANNE CETAS

Thanks be to God for his indescribable gift!

2 CORINTHIANS 9:15

Here is a hopeful thought in an increasingly chaotic world: This could be the year Jesus returns.

JOE STOWELL

We who are still alive and are left will . . . meet the Lord in the air. And so we will be with the Lord forever.

1 THESSALONIANS 4:17

We are not alone in our experience of pain. The One with nail-scarred hands is near. He will comfort us and teach us in our suffering.

DENNIS FISHER

I know, LORD, that your laws are righteous, and that in faithfulness you have afflicted me.

PSALM 119:75

When our desire for God dominates our hearts, our minds will stay focused on ways to serve Him.

JULIE ACKERMAN LINK

Love the LORD your God with all your heart and with all your soul and with all your strength.

DEUTERONOMY 6:5

Only as our lives are built on God's strength will we be able to endure the harshness of life in a fallen world.

BILL CROWDER

Come to him, the living Stone—rejected by humans but chosen by God and precious to him.

1 PETER 2:4

There aren't enough words to tell God how much we love Him! So, let's show Him our love by surrendering our hearts and lives to follow Him.

JOE STOWELL

Hear, O Israel: The LORD our God, the LORD is one. Love the LORD your God.

DEUTERONOMY 6:4-5

This is our Father's world. Let's show Him how much we love Him by respecting it and caring for the people who populate it.

MARVIN WILLIAMS

The earth is the LORD's, and everything in it, the world, and all who live in it.

PSALM 24:1

The Holy Spirit empowers us with courageous confidence in God's trustworthiness.

XOCHITL DIXON

See, the LORD your God has
given you the land. . . .
Do not be afraid;
do not be discouraged.

DEUTERONOMY 1:21

If we see each person as Jesus did—made in God's image and worthy of His love—we'll treat everyone we meet with Christlike equality.

DAVE BRANON

She has done a beautiful thing to me.

MARK 14:6

We are God's hands, feet, and voice to further His mission. How might we—with the Spirit's help—reach out today to someone unlike us?

AMY BOUCHER PYE

A crowd came together in bewilderment, because each one heard their own language being spoken.

ACTS 2:6

Even in our darkest hours, we can rest in the assurance that we are never alone, for our loving God is with us.

RANDY KILGORE

~

Your heavenly Father feeds [the birds of the air]. Are you not much more valuable than they?

MATTHEW 6:26

God is omnipresent and
eternal. Only He can be
with us all the time,
for all time.

POH FANG CHIA

You will be scattered, each to
your own home. You will leave me all
alone. Yet I am not alone, for
my Father is with me.

JOHN 16:32

Our Daily Bread Writers

The date in parentheses indicates the writer's first appearance in *Our Daily Bread*. An asterisk notes that the writer is still an active contributor to the devotional.

James Banks (October 2015*) Pastor, Peace Church, Durham, North Carolina.

Amy Boucher Pye (February 2016*) Author and speaker, North London, England.

Dave Branon (June 1984*) Former senior editor, Discovery House.

Anne Cetas (September 2004*) Former senior content editor, *Our Daily Bread*.

Poh Fang Chia (January 2014*) Director of English content development, Our Daily Bread Ministries, Singapore.

Bill Crowder (June 2006*) Vice president of ministry content, Our Daily Bread Ministries.

Lawrence Darmani (January 2015) Ghanaian novelist and publisher.

Mart DeHaan (January 1973) Former president, Our Daily Bread Ministries.

Xochitl Dixon (April 2017*) Writer, speaker, blogger at xedixon.com, Northern California.

David Egner (January 1982) Former editor, Our Daily Bread Ministries.

Dennis Fisher (May 2005) Former research editor, Our Daily Bread Ministries.

Tim Gustafson (May 2008*) Senior content editor, *Our Daily Bread*.

C. P. Hia (April 2008) Bible teacher, Singapore.

Kirsten Holmberg (March 2017*) Writer, speaker, Boise, Idaho.

Cindy Hess Kasper (October 2006*) Former editor, Our Daily Bread Ministries.

Alyson Kieda (May 2014*) Former editor, Our Daily Bread Ministries.

Randy Kilgore (January 2011) Author, Discovery House.

Julie Ackerman Link (December 2000) Author, Discovery House.

David McCasland (May 1996) Author, Discovery House.

Elisa Morgan (August 2017*) Author and speaker; cohost of *Discover the Word* and *God Hears Her* podcast.

Keila Ochoa (March 2015) Writer for children's curriculum, Querétaro, Mexico.

Patricia Raybon (October 2018*) Author, *Our Daily Bread*.

David Roper (December 2000) Author, Discovery House; former pastor.

Jennifer Benson Schuldt (September 2010*) Technical writer, Chicago.

Joe Stowell (February 2007) Former president, Cornerstone University.

Marion Stroud (September 2014) Author, Discovery House.

Herb Vander Lugt (July 1967) Former senior research editor, Our Daily Bread Ministries.

Sheridan Voysey (March 2017*) Author and speaker, Oxford, United Kingdom.

Linda Washington (April 2017) Author of numerous books, Carol Stream, Illinois.

Marvin Williams (February 2007*) Pastor, Trinity Church, Lansing, Michigan.